South view of Aldworth church, Berkshire, when 1793. J. Carter del.

Yew Tree 1793 (J. Carter)

EARLY ORIGINS

No one knows the date of the earliest settlement at Aldworth. The parish is strategically positioned in a sheltered fold at the east end of the Berkshire Downs, where the Ridgeway, the ancient upland trade and droving route from the West, descends to the Thames crossing at Streatley for the home counties. An intact section of Grimm's Ditch near the de la Beche farm-house, half a mile south of the church, together with earthen embankments towards Basildon may mark ancient community boundaries and is further evidence of early habitation.

The oldest indication of the hamlet is the knarled old yew tree at the south of the church. An issue of Gentlemen's Magazine drew attention to it in 1798: *wonderful for its bulk, the body thereof measuring upwards of nine yards, spreading its arms to a vast extent every way; but it's once lofty head is decayed and the whole is rapidly on the decline.* The yew has survived remarkably well and still produces new growth despite being uprooted in the new-year storm of 1976. It is said to be over a thousand years old.[1]

Yew Tree 1890

By the time of the Norman Conquest the agricultural settlement of *Elleorde*, derived from two Saxon words, *eald*, meaning ancient, and *worde*, meaning place of habitation, was well established. It was recorded in the Domesday Book in 1086:

The land of Theodric the goldsmith. Theodric the goldsmith holds Elleorde of the king. He held it of king Edward [the Confessor] … There is land for 5 ploughs. On the demesne there are 2 ploughs working. There are 6 villeins and 4 cottagers with 3 ploughs. There are 4 serfs and woodland for 10 pigs. It was and is worth 100 shillings.

Yew Tree 2015

---

1 A Romano-British kiln, now in the Science Museum, was found at Woodrow's Farm, 1 mi s-w. of St Mary's, in 1935

THE NORMAN CHURCH

By the late twelfth century a simple two-cell[2] church had been built in the transitional style prevalent during the gradual change from round-arched romanesque (Norman) to pointed gothic (Early English) architecture. **The font** at the west end of the church, which is still used for baptisms, dates from that time and has witnessed more than 850 years of Christian worship in this place. The flower pot font, of which there are a number in Berkshire, is said to be modelled on the wine jars used at the biblical wedding in Cana of Galilee. The fine lancet window and the lower stage of the oblong-shaped **tower,** and much of the north wall of the nave are all that remain of the first church. The first documentary evidence tells us that a *William de Rutherwyke* was priest in 1267.

THE DE LA BECHE FAMILY:
Dramatis Personae

The history of Aldworth is inextricably bound up with the de la Beches, Berkshire land-owners and public officials, who served during the reigns of Edward I, II, and III (1272-1377). They identified closely with the monarchy - their successes and failures were closely tied to those of the kings they served during their five generations at Aldworth.

Robert de La Beche [1] came to Berkshire in the mid-thirteenth century, from the Cambridgeshire land-owning branch of the family. He lived in a moated manor house on the site of the present de la Beche farm-house, half a mile south of the church. Robert was knighted in 1278, along with a William de la Beche from Sussex. In 1261 he transferred his lands in Aldworth to his son **John [2]**, who paid taxes for Aldworth and for Compton in the 1280s.

The Norman Font 1793

John's son, **Sir Philip [3]**, founder of today's Aldworth church, was joint holder of the lands by 1282. He married **Lady Joan de la Zouche [4]** produced six sons, John, Philip, Nicholas, Edmund, Robert, and Edward, and a daughter Joan. The early years were benign under the reforming King Edward I (1272-1307), who is credited with securing Wales, establishing regular parliaments, and reforming the law. The accession of Edward II (1307-1327) changed all that. Rapid promotion of his controversial favourites brought dissension from powerful barons led by his own cousin, Thomas of Lancaster. The family supported Lancaster at an early stage in opposing arbitrary rule. Sir Philip had been Sheriff of Berkshire and Oxfordshire, then of Wiltshire, and by 1321 he was returned to parliament as a Knight for Wiltshire. His responsibilities no doubt brought him into contact with Bishop Roger Mortival of Salisbury, of which diocese Aldworth was a parish: he is named in the licence to dedicate the Aldworth chancel in 1315. Sir Philip and two sons were arrested and imprisoned in July 1322 after Lancaster's final defeat at the Battle of Boroughbridge. Edward II was deposed five years later, when father and sons were released and recovered their lands.

The Isabella Seal c. 1340

John [5], Philip's eldest son, married **Isabella de Elmridge[6]**, who came from a like-minded family, supporters of Lancaster, and by whom he had two sons and three daughters. He fought for Edward I in the Scottish wars, but was a forthright critic of Edward II. After Boroughbridge, he was incarcerated in the Tower for submitting to the king *minus civiliter quam decuit.*[3] He was released in 1327 but died the same year after his ordeal. Lady Isabella has become better known since 1871 when her silver seal was found in the de la Beche fields by a ploughman. It is now in the Reading Museum. The seal is engraved with a design including the trefoil of the effigy canopies in St Mary's and family shields of de la Beche, de la Zouche, and de

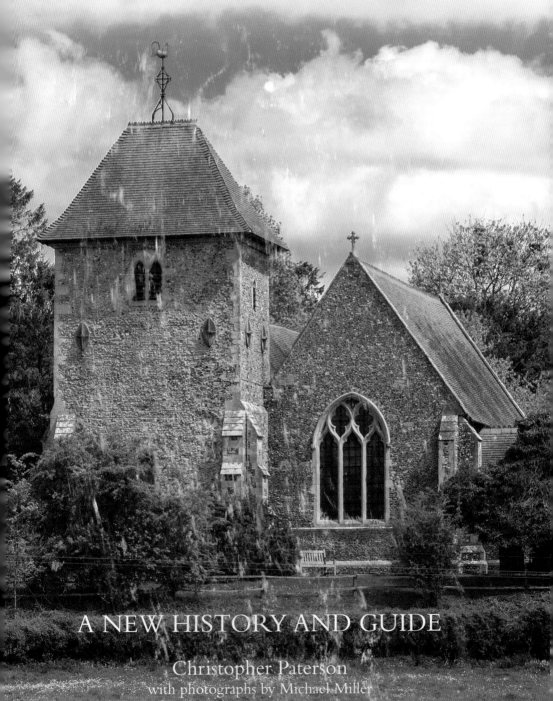

ST MARY'S CHURCH AND
THE ALDWORTH GIANTS

A NEW HISTORY AND GUIDE

Christopher Paterson
with photographs by Michael Miller

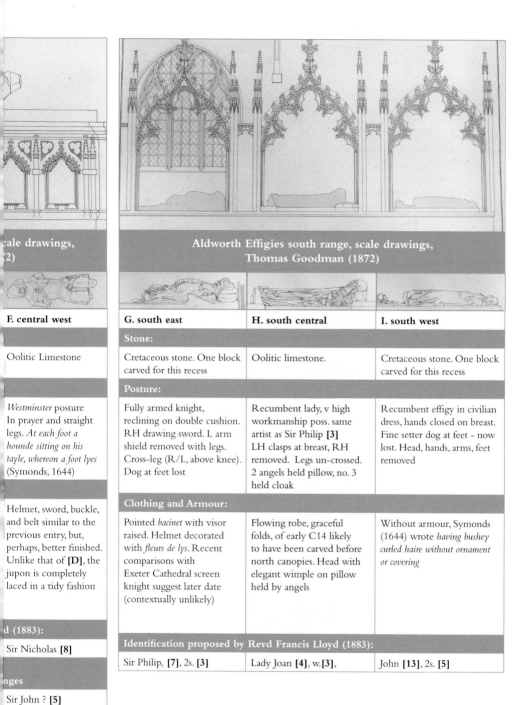

Aldworth Effigies south range, scale drawings, Thomas Goodman (1872)

F. central west	G. south east	H. south central	I. south west
	Stone:		
Oolitic Limestone	Cretaceous stone. One block carved for this recess	Oolitic limestone.	Cretaceous stone. One block carved for this recess
	Posture:		
Westminster posture In prayer and straight legs. *At each foot a hounde sitting on his tayle, whereon a foot lyes* (Symonds, 1644)	Fully armed knight, reclining on double cushion. RH drawing sword. L arm shield removed with legs. Cross-leg (R/L, above knee). Dog at feet lost	Recumbent lady, v high workmanship poss. same artist as Sir Philip [3] LH clasps at breast, RH removed. Legs un-crossed. 2 angels held pillow, no. 3 held cloak	Recumbent effigy in civilian dress, hands closed on breast. Fine setter dog at feet - now lost. Head, hands, arms, feet removed
	Clothing and Armour:		
Helmet, sword, buckle, and belt similar to the previous entry, but, perhaps, better finished. Unlike that of **[D]**, the jupon is completely laced in a tidy fashion	Pointed *bacinet* with visor raised. Helmet decorated with *fleurs de lys*. Recent comparisons with Exeter Cathedral screen knight suggest later date (contextually unlikely)	Flowing robe, graceful folds, of early C14 likely to have been carved before north canopies. Head with elegant wimple on pillow held by angels	Without armour, Symonds (1644) wrote *having bushey curled haire without ornament or covering*
	Identification proposed by Revd Francis Lloyd (1883):		
d (1883): Sir Nicholas **[8]** nges Sir John ? **[5]**	Sir Philip, **[7]**, 2s. **[3]**	Lady Joan **[4]**, w.**[3]**,	John **[13]**, 2s. **[5]**

THE ALDWORTH GIANTS

Aldworth Effigies north range scale drawings,
Thomas Goodman (1872)

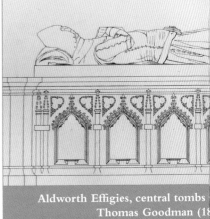

Aldworth Effigies, central tombs
Thomas Goodman (18

A. north west	B. north central	C. north east	D. central east dual	E. central east dual
Stone:			**Stone:**	
Cretaceous stone Pre-dates recess	Cretaceous stone	Oolitic limestone Not carved *in situ*	Oolitic limestone	Cretaceous stone. No stone slab.
Posture:			**Posture:**	
Cross-legged, inclined to R, head cushion. Shield L arm, R hand *pommel* (knob on hilt) of great sword. R arm, both legs, and animal at feet destroyed	Large size. 6'4" long. Double cushion L arm shield. LH sword, RH on breast. R arm and L leg broken. Fine lion next to crossed feet	*John Strong*, over life-size knight 7'2"long. Reclining position. Arms, legs crossed. Broken feet, supported by dwarf page – to emphasise size	*Westminster* posture In prayer and straight legs. Part sliced off head re-joined in 2013. Same sculptor as **[F]** Hound at each leg lion at feet	Lady is lying inclined towards knight. No head. Feet rest on animal. Despite much damage, clothing detail of great interest
Clothing and Armour:			**Clothing and Armour:**	
Plated armour with long surcoat cut short at front, kept in place by 2 belts over shoulders. Mail under shirt visible without definition	*Bacinet*, light pointed helmet decorated; *camail*, neck and shoulder; *cyclas,* long coat; *hauberk*, long chain mail, *hacketon*, leather garment; long sword, *greaves* legs; *sollarets*, feet; spurs	Early C14 armour. Round helmet, visor. Leather armour embossed rosettes, *fleurs-de-lys*. Mantle over *cylcas* and *hauberk* with folds. Light detail suggests it was highly coloured with gesso finish	*Bacinet, camail,* helmet for pillow, sword and belt, and *rowelled* (sharp tooth-wheeled) spurs. *Jupon* (sleeveless padded tunic) untidily laced, lower part pleated. Legs protected by *greaves*	Lady's dress typical of mid C14: Close fitting underdress, thrown-back mantle, dress caught up under L arm, LH on breast holds tie of cloak, RH holds up dress folds, sleeves long, decorative flaps
Identification proposed by Revd Francis Lloyd (1883):			**Identification proposed by Revd Francis Llo**	
Sir Robert **[1]**	Sir John **[2]**	Sir Philip **[3]**	Sir John **[5]**	Lady Isabella **[6]**
			Identification proposed by Mr John Grace (Richard Symonds,1644) and consequent ch	
			Sir Nicholas **[8]**	Lady Margaret ? **[9]**

INTRODUCTION

Welcome to St Mary's Church and the Aldworth Giants.

The Giants are a unique collection of life size sculptures of fourteenth-century knights. There is no other family group as large as this in any other English parish church - they are the foremost medieval monuments in West Berkshire. The mystery of the Giants and their exact identification remains unsolved and has attracted countless visitors over the years.

St Mary's Church, the home of the Giants, has been a place of worship for more than 850 years. It remains at the centre of a modern living village community on the Berkshire Downs. The village celebrated the Millennium by creating the tapestry, illustrated here, which has pride of place at the back of the church. It portrays the wide range of village activities with the church at the heart of them.

This new history and guide is intended to help visitors reach their own conclusions about the

Giants and St Mary's own rich history. It is based on a conscious effort to investigate original sources and to research rather than refer to previous accounts. It is written to coincide with the 700th anniversary of the licence to dedicate the altars of the newly re-built church, given by Bishop Mortival of Salisbury, at the behest of Sir Philip de la Beche and his fellow parishioners of Aldworth on 2 August 1315.

St Mary's Church and the Aldworth Giants: Plan

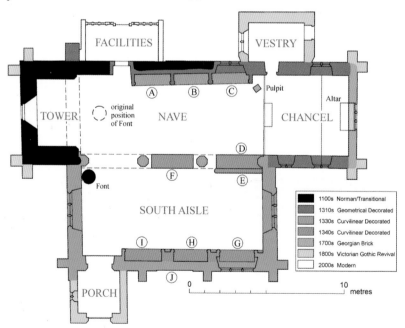

FACILITIES

VESTRY

Pulpit

Altar

TOWER

original position of Font

NAVE

CHANCEL

(A) (B) (C)

(D)

(F) (E)

Font

SOUTH AISLE

(I) (H) (G)

(J)

■	1100s Norman/Transitional
	1310s Geometrical Decorated
	1330s Curvilinear Decorated
	1340s Curvilinear Decorated
	1700s Georgian Brick
	1800s Victorian Gothic Revival
	2000s Modern

PORCH

0   10
|—————————————————| metres

Please refer to indicators [A] – [J] for effigy positions on the Church Plan.

Please refer to indicators [1] to [13] for de la Beche family members on Family Tree on p.3

Published by Sarum House Press
On behalf of St Mary's Church Aldworth PCC, Berkshire,
© Christopher Paterson, 2015
Sarum House, Upper Basildon, Berkshire, RG8 8NA
ISBN No 978-0-9933135-0-9

Elmridge (?). The discovery caused some excitement among local historians, establishing a direct link between de la Beche and the effigies. It is most likely from the years after John's death when Isabella conducted significant business on her own. Their two sons, **Thomas [12],** who died 3 years after his father in 1331, and **John [13],** who died at the age of twenty in 1336, left their three sisters as his heirs.

Philip de la Beche [7], second son of Philip **[3]**, a Knight Bachelor, was Sherriff of Berkshire and Oxford in 1332-33. After John's estates were split between him and his brother, Nicholas, they worked closely together and were licensed to empark lands in Aldworth in 1336. Philip died in 1339.

Aldworth Knight [F]

Sir Nicholas [8], third son of Philip **[3]**, was the most distinguished of the line. He was keeper of Montgomery Castle and of Plessey in Essex in the 1320s. Warrants were issued for his arrest along with his father and brothers after Buroughbridge, but he managed to escape imprisonment. The early and middle years of Edward III's reign (1327 -1377) were the high years of de la Beche influence. In 1339 the King licensed the family to crenellate their manors at de la Beche, Shinfield, and Watlington. Nicholas was then appointed Keeper of the Tower of London and became tutor to the king's eldest son, later the Black Prince. After being purged with other royal officials over their unwillingness to finance wars against France, he was quickly restored. By 1343 he was Seneschal (or Governor) of Gascony, a royal domain then about one third of the size of England, and an ambassador

to the King of Castille, whose son was to marry Edward III's daughter. Sir Nicholas led military campaigns to restore south west France and lived long enough to celebrate the Black Prince's victory at the Battle of Crecy in 1346. He had no children by his wife, **Lady Margaret [9]**, who married for the third time within a year of his death.

Edmund de la Beche [10], a cleric and soldier, once involved in the seizure of Wallingford castle, was last of the line. He held public office and was Archdeacon of Berkshire. After his death in 1365, no member of the family lived at de la Beche.

The estates devolved to his sister **Joan [11]**, wife of Sir John de Langford of Bradfield, whose family held them until the sixteenth century. It was noted by Sheldon as early as 1678, that of the crenellated manor house, *no ruines now remain*.

DE LA BECHE OF ALDWORTH FROM C.1250 TO 1382

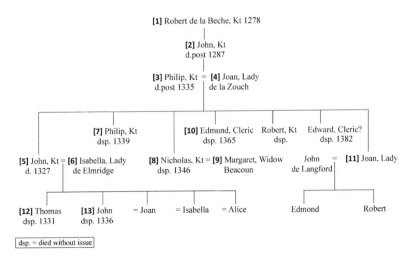

ew in Aldworth church, looking east [divested of the pews,] taken 179 **The Medieval Nave (J. Carter, 1793)**

THE NEW CHANCEL AND THE NAVE - 1315

The wave of church building in the thirteenth and fourteenth centuries marked the emergence of the English Church from the post-conquest period and a desire for higher, lighter, and more modern churches. The new churches catered for new needs – the increasing preoccupation with the after-life and obituaries, special devotions to St Mary, and more complex rites requiring more clergy round the altar at Mass.

The building of a new church was, then as now, a statement of the patron's faith and influence in the community and of the church's liturgy and teaching to the worshippers. By the early 1300s three generations of de la Beche knights had prospered in

Aldworth. With Sir Philip elected Sheriff, they were one of the more prominent families in the county. The idea of re-building the church for their parish of Aldworth would have been a natural one. The licence to consecrate the altars of their new church, which followed, happily survives in Bishop Roger Mortival's Register.

LICENCE FOR THE DEDICATION OF THE ALTARS. [2 August, 1315]

To the venerable in Christ our Lord by the grace of God Bishop of Menevia, Roger, by divine approval chosen and confirmed Bishop of Sarum [sends] the reverence and honour due to such a worthy Father.

C15 Choir stall end

Licence to dedicate the altars, 2 August 1315

Moved by the prayers of our beloved in Christ Philip de la Beche, parishioner of the Church of Aldworth in the diocese of Salisbury, and the other fellow parishioners of the said church, asking that you should have the power of consecrating the altars of the said church, we grant you in the name of the Lord, by this present document, the full faculty [for such consecrating]. May your reverence long remain in health

Given at Noseley on the first Saturday after the Feast of St Peter in Chains, in the year etc.[4]

Sir Philip's new chancel is still in its original form, apart from the east wall replaced in 1740. The window tracery of the chancel is typical of the 'geometrical Decorated' style of the first two decades of the 1300s.

The south wall has a quinquefoil headed two stage *piscina* with a circular basin of attractive design and two stone seats [*sedilia*] of different heights set into the deep sill of the eastern window. The head of this window is more ornate than those of the other two chancel windows and retains part of its medieval red and white glass. The *sedilia* suggest that there would have been more than one priest at the celebration of communion on Sundays.

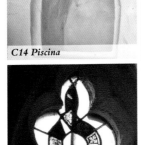

C14 Piscina

C14 glass

The chancel had an exquisite fifteenth-century timber screen, which separated the chancel from the nave. Two fragments of the woodwork have been recovered, two cinque-foiled pieces built into the vestry cupboard and a four-centred arch with spandrels in the roof of the nineteenth-century lych-gate. Both indicate a high standard of workmanship. The whole chancel was evidently spacious, light, and finely decorated and would have been planned for the developing ceremonial of the Salisbury diocese, *the rite of Sarum*, which was then becoming the standard in many parts of the English Church.

A finely sculptured stone figure (said to be the Lord at the day of judgement) was found hidden in brickwork below the west window of the south aisle in 1845. It may originally have been positioned in a medieval carved stone reredos behind the altar or on the corbel bracket of the eastern respond of the central arcade. The statue was returned to the church in 1884, but sadly disappeared from a display in the church in the 1980s.

Three ancient *poppy-head* bench ends have survived, now at the back of the nave. These have been dated by experts to the late fifteenth century. Recent examination by Hugh Harrison concluded that the original position of their book board fixings and the absence of front panels indicate

C14 screen work

that these ends were attached to the medieval choir stalls. John Carter, the antiquarian's pen and wash drawing of 1793 shows that the ends were attached to stalls in the chancel at that time. The three newer bench ends are fine nineteenth-century reproductions.

The illustrations also show four decorated fourteenth-century tiles. Aldworth is the only known parish church in which John Carter recorded tiles,

C14 tiles (J. Carter, 1793)

the rest of his work on tiles being in Cathedrals. Laurence Keen has shown that the rampant lion quatre-foil design is similar to tiles in the Carfax, Oxford and in Eynsham Abbey, while the quarter-tile of a double lined circle with fleurs-de-lys is like tiles from Uffington, Berkshire and from Dorchester Abbey. While Carter's drawings are impressionistic, they indicate that the floors were laid with tiles of considerable quality from a regional workshop.

It is likely that the wide tower arch is of the fourteenth century – its design is contemporary, with simple chamfering similar to that elsewhere in the nave. It is evident from their advanced design that the effigy canopies of the nave were built later than the chancel, in the 1330s.

4 The licence was addressed to the Bishop of Menevia, the ancient name for St David's in Wales. David Martin the bishop had been appointed suffragan of Reading, responsible for Aldworth. Bishop Roger Mortival had just been appointed to Salisbury and was part resident at Noseley in Leicestershire, where his family chapel still exists. The feast of St Peter's Chains on 1st August is still celebrated in parts of the Anglican communion and there is a church of that dedication in the City of London.

Canopy Cusps

Comic head stop

Curvilinear reticulations and mouldings

Canopy pinnacles

The South Aisle and canopies, 1330s–40s

THE NEW SOUTH AISLE AND THE CANOPIES, 1330s

The restoration of the de la Beche family to their lands and privileges in 1327and the continuing preferment of Sir Nicholas under Edward III marked the heyday of a family who had prospered in the century since they arrived in Aldworth. The remarkable success of the family in successive generations, in a society and church increasingly preoccupied by death, remembrance, and the after-life, was the backdrop to the dramatic plan to expand the church with an impressive new south aisle. The church was re-ordered to provide exquisitely canopied tombs of the latest designs for a suite of finely carved monumental effigies. The aim was to provide a showplace for their achievements and a setting for intercessions for the family departed.

It is difficult to imagine the south aisle chapel as it must have been when first commissioned. The reformation and the civil war have taken their toll on the effigies, the bright medieval colours of the monuments have long since disappeared, the open floors are now filled with pews, and the wall decorations have been whitewashed over. Despite all this, the south aisle remains an impressive light-filled space in which the mutilated figures still set the scene. Unusually, the aisle of 18ft 3ins (5.48m) is wider than the nave of 16ft 3ins (4.95m): they are separated by a triple-arch arcade supported by octagonal piers typical of the 1330s. The importance of the aisle is emphasised by multiple hood mouldings on the aisle side of the arches, enlivened by two grotesque canine head stops. As Pevsner pointed out, the dog heads appear to be *straight out of a modern comic.*

Within the east bay of the arcade, two bracket openings in the stonework above the pier capitals above and adjacent to the dual tomb indicate that a timber screen separated the aisle from the nave, at the east of the archway. The corbel stone at the head of the east respond was evidently to hold a sculpted figure.

In the short few years since the building of the chancel, the English Decorated style had moved on from 'geometric' to 'curvilinear' tracery which was for several decades at the forefront of European architecture. As a result the three large east, south, and west windows of the new south aisle have advanced tracery designs with large ogee (S-curved) reticulations and mouldings at the top of the three-light windows. These are complemented by the two ranges of elaborate canopies at the north and south walls of the church. The cutting-edge features of the two ranges show that they were built some years apart. The earlier north range has a single buttress between each arch topped by a crenelated pinnacle, with stiff leaf capitals on attached columns, typical of early fourteenth-century work, and may have pre-dated the south work by ten years or so. The later south range has two buttresses between each arch topped with gables and multiple pinnacles, and the canopy traceries, with their (much restored) tensile open work, must date from the early1340s.

THE GIANTS

The early fourteenth century was a key period in the development of English monumental sculpture. Rather flat twelfth and thirteenth century effigies, first developed in Tournai marble and later in English Purbeck 'marble', were being replaced by figures in soft English limestone which was easier to work. The availability of pliable limestone made delicate under-cutting possible, bright coloured painting more natural, and off site figure carving viable. This was a brief window of opportunity before the 'Black Death' (1349-50) after which the shortage of craftsmen made *in situ* sculpture work more expensive and the advent of alabaster figure work followed. It is not surprising that in this period newly established knightly families such as the de la Beches of Berkshire, the Alards of Winchelsea, and the Hautevilles of Chew Magna in Somerset made their mark in local parish churches, while the wealthier baronial dynasties (such as the Percys, Dispencers, and Berkeleys) held sway in the great churches (such as Beverley, Tewkesbury, and St. Augustine's Abbey, Bristol).

The 'Giants' consist of nine, formerly ten, life-size knightly effigies of the fourteenth century. While the sculptures seem quite forlorn in their dilapidated state, they still constitute sculpture of great merit. What makes these monuments unique is that there is no single family group as large as this in any other English parish church. It is remarkable that no inscription, heraldry, or document has survived which can provide sufficient evidence to identify them. As a result numerous distinguished visitors over the centuries have illustrated and researched them: but a convincing definition of their individual identities has always eluded them.

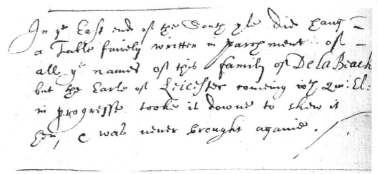

Elizabeth I (Millennium Tapestry)

The Queen's visit (Richard Symonds, 1644)

ELIZABETH 1, THE CIVIL WAR
AND THE LEGEND OF THE GIANTS

Richard Symonds, an ordinary soldier in the royal army of Charles I, visited Aldworth on 2 May, 1644. He was a clerk in the chancery court with a personal interest in heraldry. His *diaries of the great civil war* were written during the frequent gaps in the military campaigns, when he also found time to record heraldic inscriptions and monuments. Although there was no heraldry, his visit to Aldworth was highly rewarding, and his descriptions of the effigies are now in the British Library.

While Symonds found nothing to identify the effigies, he took note of local folklore:

The common people called the statues John Long, John Strong, John Neverafraid and John Everafraid. They call ye statue outside of the Churche, John Everafraid, and say further he gave his soule to the Divil, if ever he was buried either in the Churche, or Churchyard; so he was buryed under the Churche wall under an arche.

Symonds drew sketches of three effigies – the over-size knight to the east of the north range **[C]**, the so-called *John Strong*, and the knight and lady on the dual tomb under the easternmost central arch **[D&E]**, which he captioned *Sir Nicholas de la Beach*, adding *as Mr Grace the Incumbent told me.* John Grace had been inducted to the parish as early as 1619, and he was able to recount the visit to Aldworth of Queen Elizabeth (1559-1603) and her favourite, the Earl of Leicester, which had been within the living memory of some of his older parishioners.

In ye East ende of ye South yle did hang a Table fairly written in Parchment of all ye names of ye family of De

la Beach; but ye Earle of Leicester, coming with ye Queen Elizabeth in progresse, tooke it down to shew it her, and [it] was never brought againe.

The Queen was said to have travelled on horseback on a pillion behind the Earl on one of her royal progresses or country house tours. They may have been staying at Ewelme Manor, twelve miles away, a favoured royal residence since the 1540s, where Elizabeth and her sister, Mary, had spent carefree childhood holidays together.

After Symond's visit, the royal armies were rebuffed at Reading, and retreated along the Pang valley through 'Inglefield' (17 May) and 'Bradley' to Compton (18 May). Here *on the top of the playne hills, was the rendezvous of the whole army that Satterday.* The rebels took Abingdon ten days later and, after Waller brought 10,000 men and 150 horses into play, the King abandoned Oxford retreating to Worcester which he reached on 6 June.

King Charles was executed in 1649. The date of the mutilation and defacement of the Aldworth giants is not known. The new vicar, Thomas Longland resigned shortly after his induction in 1658, *because (as he caused to be written in the register) he would not accede to the sacrilege and wickedness of his people.*

In 1666, the College of Arms, seeking to regulate heraldry in the years after the Civil War, sent Elias Ashmole, the Windsor Herald and a well-known antiquarian, and Edward Bysshe, King of Arms. Like Symonds, they were disappointed by the absence of heraldry, but produced a fine set of

8

drawings, the first after the destruction, which is still held at the college.

There was considerable interest in the monuments in the 1790s. John Carter visited in 1793 with his draughtsman, George Basire - his finely detailed colour wash drawings are now in the Gough collection at Oxford. I. Stone drew the interior in 1797 for publication in the *Gentleman's Magazine* leading to an extended correspondence about the merits and importance of the effigies in 1798 and 1799. *An Architect* enthused that the *John Strong* statue *has on exquisite rich armour, and partakes of every requisite to render it equal to any piece of sculpture of Greece or Rome.*

No further discussion is on record until 1844, when William Hewett, an East Ilsley antiquarian, wrote his admirable *History of the Antiquities of the Hundred of Compton.* However his assumption that *five effigies which are cross legged must be distinguished ancestors, crusaders. all of whom died before the year 1310* was wrong. W.S. Walworth wrote a commentary in 1857, accompanied by a fine scale drawing of the *John Strong* effigy by Edward Blore, a former Surveyor of Westminster Abbey (1827-1849). He surmised that the aisle was a family mausoleum of the second quarter of the fourteenth century based on the date of its canopies.

Francis Llewelyn Lloyd became vicar in 1857. Although an earlier 1845 restoration of the church had improved the facilities, the canopied effigies were in a shocking state. Lloyd commissioned Thomas Goodman, an Oxford architect, to produce scale drawings of the effigies and canopies. Goodman's drawings, reproduced here[5], were very crisp. By 1883, Lloyd had completed his own historical research which was published as a 16 page article accompanied by miniatures of Thomas Goodman's drawings. He was careful to label his work an *attempt to identify* the giants, and simply listed all the members of the de la Beche family from about 1250 to 1382 followed by the details of the effigy by which he had concluded they were represented. However, by the time of the visit of the Newbury Field Club two years later, Lloyd was more assertive in quoting his identifications as fact.

The Church Monuments Society has insisted that it is not possible to identify the effigies without documentary evidence, but suggests that the last word has not been said.

'John Strong' (Richard Symonds, 1644)

Sir Nicholas de la Beach (Richard Symonds, 1644)

INTERPRETING THE 'GIANTS': CONTEXT, HISTORY, AND THE RECORD

Please refer to indicators **[A]** – **[J]** for effigy positions on the Church Plan opposite p.1.

Please refer to indicators **[1]** to **[13]** for de la Beche family members on Family Tree on p.3

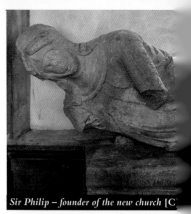
Sir Philip – founder of the new church [C]

Recent guides have tended to follow Francis Lloyd's identification scheme of 1883 despite the Church Monuments Society view. This section will follow the evidence more closely.

That the stone carvings are of different periods is shown by the posture of the effigies, their armour and weapons, and changes in dress and costume. At least five have been moved from their original positions, and four stand out for their distinctive workmanship and the use of high grade oolitic limestone.

Two of the statues have long been recognised. The giant-sized knight, known variously as *John Strong* and as *the dying Gaul*, is identified by Lloyd as Sir Philip de la Beche **[3]**, founder of the new church, and is carved in exquisite detail. It can be dated as early C14. Arthur Gardner, the medieval sculpture expert, noted that as the century progressed military effigies began to strike more active poses, as is shown here. The work was not carved within its present recess **[C]**, and its position on the north side nearest to the altar - traditionally the founder's position - makes Lloyd's attribution probable. His larger-than-life size at 7'2" (2184 mm), accentuated by his diminutive, now headless, page boy, adds to the sense of his importance.

Probably Lady Jane, wife of Sir Philip [H]

The other much discussed figure, identified by Lloyd as Lady Joan **[4]**, wife of Sir Philip **[3]**, lies in her wimple and deeply folded drapes, her head resting on a cushion formerly supported by angels, but now consigned to the centre canopy among the odd men out of the south range **[H]**. Gardner drew attention to its similarity to Alexander of Abingdon's statue of Queen Eleanor at Waltham Cross, carved in the 1290s. This pair of monuments is of exceptional workmanship and may be the work of one sculptor. Both have been moved and if the attributions are correct, would have been in one place in an earlier display.

Aldworth Knight – Sir John or Sir Nicholas

Two more statues stand out, probably of the brothers identified by Lloyd as the second Sir John **[5]** and Sir Nicholas **[8]**, first and third sons of Sir Philip **[3]**. These are confident knightly effigies in the supplicatory posture described by Gardner as *mid-century Westminster,* the character of whose faces is interchangeable. They wear the pointed *bacinets* typical of a generation later, and they too were likely carved by one artist, from limestone similar to that of the previous pair. Each is mounted on one of the central plinths **[D]** and **[F]**. That identified as Sir John shares a dual tomb with a lady effigy, presumed to be that of his wife Lady Isabella **[6]** **[E]**.

Lloyd identified the central effigy on the central tomb **[F]** in solitary splendour under the middle arch as that of Sir Nicholas de la Beche **[8]**. However this cannot be reconciled with

Sir Nicholas or Sir John - and Lady [D&E]

Richard Symonds' 1644 sketch of the effigies of the eastern dual tomb **[D&E]**, which clearly labels the knight as *Sir Nicolas de Beche, as Mr Grace the Incumbent told me.* Lloyd must have been familiar with Richard Symonds account, documented by Hewett in 1844, but had either not seen the original text or perhaps chosen to ignore it. For Lloyd, the 1871 discovery of the Isabella seal was the key piece of evidence connecting the de la Beche family to the canopies *for until lately there was no clue to the persons commemorated.* Thus Lloyd's scheme identifies Lady Isabella in the place of honour on the dual tomb **[E]**; but should the effigy on the dual tomb **[D]** be Sir Nicholas, his accompanying lady **[E]** would have to be Lady Margaret **[9]**. Whoever the Lady, this statue is finely worked - the thrown back mantle, drawn-up drapes, and decorative flaps, are reckoned to date from mid-century and contrast with the earlier style worn by Lady Joan **[4]**. After Sir John's death in 1327 the eastern dual tomb would have been more appropriate for Sir Nicholas as he gained power and influence, being closer to the altar. The two statues were originally surrounded by elaborate screens and imagery, which must have attracted the most severe mutilation from the Civil War wreckers.

The older figures under the north west **[A]** and north centre **[B]** canopies were identified by Lloyd as Sir Robert **[1]** and his son, the first Sir John **[2]**, in logical progression to the easternmost canopy **[C]** of his grandson, Sir Philip **[3]**. This leaves the south range, the last to be filled, in which the second Sir Philip **[7]** of the fourth generation, second son of the first Sir Philip **[3]**, was identified by Lloyd with the effigy under the south east canopy **[G]**, and John **[13]**, of the fifth generation, second son of Sir John **[5]** with the south west canopy **[I]**, leaving Lady Joan **[4]** placed awkwardly between them **[H]**.

Edmund, Archdeacon of Berkshire and last in the line, died nearly twenty years later than Sir Nicholas in 1365. It is thought that he may have tried to found a collegiate chapel for the south aisle to preserve the dynastic memory. Lloyd tells us that beneath the floor of the south aisle is a large Purbeck slab with inlaid stone borders with a half-length brass of a medieval cleric. This is a more likely monument for Edmund in the period after the Black Death.

There remains the tenth effigy **[J]** to complete the story. In 1678, the effigy known as *John Everafraid* was still under an arch in the outside wall of the church. Sheldon noted that there *lies ye statue of a man in armour, cross-legged, at this present almost even with the ground.* John Carter's drawing of the south view of the church in 1793[6] shows the effigy still present, but by the time of Hewett's *History* in 1844 it had been bricked up.

The south aisle chapel and the de la Beche canopies remain as a memorial to four generations of ambitious and distinguished knights, who based their lives at their moated manor house in Aldworth in the thirteenth and fourteenth centuries. As they gained fame, they completed a magnificent chapel to honour their departed and for intercession on their behalf by succeeding generations. The family's opposition to Edward II had seriously weakened the family inheritance and the successive deaths of each of Sir Philip's sons without male issue meant that no permanent chantry or college could be founded to continue the memory.

6 see page 1

THE GEORGIAN CHURCH

The restoration of the monarchy in 1660 marked a turning point for the church. A painted royal coat of arms bearing the date was hung above the tower arch, and in 1669 a local squire, John Whistler, Gent., was buried in the traditional position at the centre of the nave facing the altar, a ledger-stone proudly displaying his coat of arms. In 1691, the Revd Jonathon Davidson refused to recognise the deposition of the anointed King James II, and was ejected after refusing to swear allegiance to William III (one of 400 clergy who did so).

By the second quarter of the eighteenth century new patterns of worship were established and the church was radically re-modelled to reflect the new social order. The style of the new church was unashamedly auditory rather than sacramental, reflecting the hall-like design of new churches which became the norm in the era of Sir Christopher Wren. It no longer emphasised the liturgical progression from nave, to choir, to altar as medieval churches did; the intention was to maximise the seated area available for the congregation to hear readings and preaching.

Seating plan for Aldworth Church, 1743

Seating was arranged in comfortable box pews which were reserved for their owners or tenants.

In Aldworth, the east chancel wall and its medieval window were replaced with newly fashionable brick and a round-arch plain glass window, after the manner of that at Stanford Dingley (1768). A simple external stone plaque in the brickwork marked the date of 1740.[5] The centre of worship moved to the larger south aisle, which was provided with box pews throughout and a western gallery *for the choristers* which had four rows of seating above the west end of the aisle. The fine pulpit, thought to date from 1639, was purchased from St. Laurence, Reading in 1742. A lectern and prayer desk, more domestic and of later date, were acquired to complete the suite. Whitewashed timbered ceilings were inserted below the roof, which Carter noted was modern in 1793, to improve acoustics and heating. The nave was largely empty, as it was out of the sight line of the preacher, but pews and boxes were retained on the north side of the nave, which was more visible. This left an open space at the back of the nave, with the font towards its centre.

The accounts for the modernisation of the church, signed by the Vicar, George Deane, make interesting reading, and amounted to £50 14s 11½d (£50.75p). Half of the expenses (£25) were borne by the patron, the second Earl of Abingdon, who like the de la Beches, 400 years before, had been member for Berkshire and Oxfordshire and Constable of the Tower. Abingdon was a peer and lord justice,

Pulpit, 1639, acquired 1742

7 The present re-covered stone appears to say 1701. Hewett recorded it as 1740 in 1844, which is much more likely.

an absentee landlord, whose country house was near Thame – his interests were represented by his chief tenant, Edward Bartholomew of Dummer (Dunworth) Farm. The parishioners collected a further £17, while St John's College, Cambridge, the ecclesiastical patron paid a further £5.

On completion of the work a meeting of parishioners was held for ye *Disposal of ye Seats because ye Lord Abingdon had so very generously contributed towards ye building of them*. The account of the meeting gives a unique insight into the workings of the community. It was put to Farmer Bartholomew *to choose what seat he liked best*. After he had elected to take not only the new patron's box but also to retain his traditional place in the nave, there were objections from Mr Cheney, who rented the largest farm in the village at Pibworth and who had a larger family. A negotiated settlement allowed Farmer Bartholomew to build a grander box pew in his old position at the head of the nave, immediately across the dual tomb from, and close to, the Minister and Parish Clerk - *Ye Seat is now much ye largest and ye best in ye whole Church*. Farmer Cheney occupied the superior new patron's box A in the aisle, with Farmer Lewendon, who rented the next largest farm, in box B. The remainder of the boxes on each side were allocated to tenants and owners according to the size of their holdings or to their contribution for their seat. Towards the back on the right hand side was *Matt Bacon, a Shoemaker, who lives in one of Lord Abingdon's Houses which he rents from Farmer Bartholomew* and on the left hand side, *W. Force, a poor labouring man, but who has an House and a little close of his own, who pays a small matter to ye Poor Rate and also an old woman and wife of a carpenter.*

At the end of the meeting, the Parish Clerk summed up,

Y Farmers in y Parish have professd Themselves satisfyd at their siting where they do.

George Deane employed a curate, Richard Graves, the following year, but was unable to accommodate him, as the Vicarage was undergoing building works at the time. Edward Bartholomew took in the young curate, an ordained Fellow of All Souls, then 31 years old, in the nearby Dummer Farmhouse. There Graves fell in love with his younger daughter, Lucy (16), and secretly married her in London a few weeks before the birth of their first child. As his biographer put it, *the marriage lost him his fellowship and offended his relations*. However it did not prevent Graves being presented a few years later to the rectory of Claverton near Bath over which he presided for more than 50 years and where he became an accomplished writer.

Grave's best known work, a light humoured satire, *The Spiritual Quixote* (1772), is not irrelevant to Aldworth, and it established his reputation as a picaresque novelist. During his first years at Claverton, Graves lost part of his congregation to an itinerant preacher, a shoemaker. The central character, Geoffrey Wildgoose, was his Methodist *Don Quixote*, who having a grievance against his parson, went out to convert the world with Gerry Tugwell, his *Sancho Panza*. The story reached its climax when Wildgoose was injured in the head by a pitcher of wine thrown by a disbeliever: fortunately his ailments were slight and he lived happily ever after. The story was based on Graves' experiences in Bath, but there were those in Aldworth who likened *Gerry Tugwell* to Matt Bacon, the shoemaker, and *Mr Woodville* to Edward Bartholomew, both box-holders in the re-modelled Parish Church.

Interior of the church, 1797 (I. Stone)

Richard Graves, curate, 1744-46

VICTORIAN ALDWORTH

The *long eighteenth century* was a period of stability and prosperity. George Deane, vicar for 48 years, handed over to Henry Hetley, incumbent for 50 years. Hetley was also vicar of Wilton and a prebendary of Salisbury Cathedral. After a long period of relative inactivity, the parish was ready for change. Increases in farming output required more labour and the population of Aldworth, 305 at the 1841 census, peaked at 350 in 1871. National concern that provision should be made for the rapidly expanding working classes brought well over 150,000 additional seats in new and expanded churches by 1840. The coming of the Great Western in 1841, just 3 miles away, brought investment of £60,000 on Moulsford and Gatehampton bridges, much of which was spent on local brick work.

By 1832, when Revd John Austen arrived, the Georgian re-modelling was no longer fit for purpose - reflecting the social order and village numbers of a century before. His early years were marked by high minded social initiatives including the new school, a Sunday School, and the Clothing Club. The last was a popular venture - members were *labouring people residing in the parish, married or single, male or female* - 43 families were members by 1853. A new library had 47 titles - the most-borrowed were *Pears Companion*, and *Pilgrim's Progress*.

Spurred on by the building of a Primitive Methodist Chapel in 1835, Austen turned his attention to reorganising the church for greater numbers. In 1845, the outmoded box pews and gallery were abandoned, and the pulpit and clerk's desk moved to the head of the nave, which reverted to being the centre of Sunday worship. New pews and a new heating system were installed throughout- enough for 180 parishioners. The burial vaults were bricked up by 1844 and a new coffin house constructed. The renewal was not confined to facilities and in 1846 Austen was able to present no less than 28 parishioners for confirmation by the Bishop.

Francis Lloyd established the church in the form we have it today between 1857 and 1888. While the 1840s refurbishment improved facilities, the building itself was decaying. Lloyd recognised that the Giants could be used to popularise Aldworth and to attract new donors. His visitors' book shows his engagement with prominent churchmen, politicians, archaeologists, and architects throughout his term. This was hugely successful and the 1870 and 71 building accounts show his financial support came not only from the Aldworth manors, the Benyons of Englefield, and the Morrisons of Basildon, but also from a duke, a cabinet minister, bishops, MPs, numerous clergy, and a later Edward Bartholomew.

The 1870s restoration by J.P. St Aubyn was intended to restore quality of worship and to make the church more sympathetic to its Decorated roots. The chancel was cleared for more traditional Communion by moving the choir stalls back to the nave. To make way for the new vestry, the medieval screen was replaced by the present Decorated-style one. The crucifix above is Italian work, purchased at a later date. It is unclear when the 1740 east window was replaced by the present decorated-style window, rather plain compared with the medieval work: an early photo shows it in position before the new vestry was built. St Aubyn made his mark with his distinctive, rather Germanic, tower. It has a treble bell and a second of 1868 by Mears and Stainbank, a tenor by Rt & Is Wells of Aldbourne of 1793, and a call bell of 1635. A new crown-post roof with braces for the south aisle was probably introduced at this time, and a new porch and the lych-gate of 1878, designed by Sir Gilbert Scott, were added.

Restoration of the canopies based on Goodman's large-scale drawings of 1869 was by Thomas Earp, best known for his 1863 reconstruction of the Eleanor Cross at Charing Cross. He handled much of the carving work offsite at his workshops in Lambeth. The work has been criticised by Pevsner as *terribly over-restored*. However the south range was in a ruinous state and the eastern canopy, which had been removed before 1793, had to be re-made entirely. The work on the north range work is more sympathetic.

The new stained glass of the east window was commissioned in 1921 in memory of parishioners who had lost their lives in World War I. The glass was designed and made by John Bewsey, a pupil of Charles Kempe, in his English fifteenth-century style. It portrays Christ crucified with St Mary and St John in the upper roundel with the shields of the Province and the Diocese to the left and right. The main range of three lights portrays St Peter to the left, St Mary with the baby Jesus in the centre, and St George to the right. The style of the architectural canopies which form the backdrop to the figures is fourteenth-century as befits the church.

The charming early twentieth-century Nativity reredos in plaster, now in need of conservation, was fashioned by Margaret Watson, daughter and one of ten children of Revd A. L. Watson, vicar from 1918 to 1936.

WORLD WARS

The First World War took a considerable toll on Aldworth and the names of the eleven men who lost their lives are recorded on the village War Memorial. This is a stone plaque in the place of honour on the east wall of the church, where they are honoured each year on Remembrance Sunday.

One in six of the households recorded in the 2011 census lost husbands or sons. Their occupations show that all but one of the nine men who also appear in census records were from the agricultural mainstream of the parish. Arthur Goodchild (18, in 1914), born in Quick's Green, was a carter, as were Edwin Greenaway (28) and Thomas Lovelock (51). Charles Smith, also 51, was a farm labourer as was William Pinfold (17); and Albert Hall (33) a builder's labourer. The brothers, James (22) and Jesse (20) Marcham were a domestic under gardener and an under shepherd, the eldest sons of James Marcham (46), a head shepherd, who had 6 sons and 4 daughters. Lucy Marcham (63), a widow and probably their grandmother, worked at the Bell, where she worked for Georgina McQhae (69), the Inn Keeper. Villiers Middleton (29), born in Goring, was a house painter by trade at the time of the census.

Laurence Binyon, war poet, 1869-1943, by William Strang

War memorial

Laurence Binyon's gravestone, where his ashes were scattered, is against the hedge to the north of the church-yard.

The Second World War brought further losses: four men of Aldworth are named on the memorial. The Dunlop family, who lived in de la Beche from 1930, lost their two sons. Both served on Royal Family protection duties in the Castle Company of the Grenadier Guards at Windsor: Brian (21, on his date of death) died on night patrol in Tunisia in 1943, and Hugh (20), was shot avoiding capture by the Germans near Florence, in 1944.

Laurence Binyon, the war poet and a keeper of documents at the British Museum, spent his retirement years at Westridge Green from 1933 to 1943. At the outset of the First World War he was too old to enlist but worked as a hospital orderly in Haut-Marne and later near Verdun. In retirement, he was Norton Professor of Poetry at Harvard and continued his academic work at Trinity College, Oxford. He is best known for *For the Fallen* which was written in September 1914, following the Battle of the Marne. The fourth stanza is that traditionally read at Remembrance Sunday services:

They shall grow not old, as we that are left grow old:
Age shall not weary them, nor the years condemn,
At the going down of the sun, and in the morning
We will remember them.

...mas Service, 2014

ST MARY'S TODAY

This history is of a church which has continuously transformed itself to reflect both the wishes of its patrons and those of local parishioners. Each new era of construction, Norman, Decorated, Georgian, and Victorian - as well as the destruction of the Civil War - has left its mark on St Mary's - as a statement for the local community and as a text for the congregation.

The late twentieth century changed Aldworth from an agricultural settlement, which it had been for centuries, to a base for people working in a wide range of services throughout the county and beyond. With a smaller population, the school numbers reduced to 4 per year, leading to its closure in 1961, and the parish joined in a united benefice with neighbouring Ashampstead and Basildon. The parish maintains a regular pattern of Sunday services throughout the year and the church is open every day. The parishioners arrange a series of events each year including concerts, talks, and summer teas in the churchyard, which form part of the wider activities of the village.

The fabric has been well cared for with a comprehensive external restoration in 1984, the addition of an extension with kitchen and toilet facilities in 2012, and a delicate restoration of the canopies and Giants, with the generous support of local trusts and donations.

The seven hundredth anniversary of the church in 2015 has brought with it renewed optimism, new forms of inclusive service, a wider programme of events, and a plan for a new permanent interpretative exhibition on the Giants at St Mary's at the rear of the church. All of this will contribute to transforming the church once again for the needs of the twenty-first century.

Go in Peace
May the love of the Father enfold you,
The wisdom of the Son enlighten you,
And the fire of the Spirit kindle you:
And may the blessing of the Lord God
be with you today and always.

Acknowledgements: Special thanks are due to Michael Miller who has taken most of the photographs in this booklet and to Stuart Anderson of Fine Print who designed it. Thanks also to Duncan Craig of Fine Print, Witney, for arranging the printing. My thanks to the staff of the Berkshire Record Office, the Bodleian Library, the British Library, the Reading Museum, and the Wiltshire and Swindon Archives for assisting with access to original sources. I am grateful to Professor John Cottingham for his translation of the Aldworth Licence, to Tony Ives for his work on the Plan and the Family Tree, and to Sarah Darling (nee Dunlop), Jill Greenaway, Hugh Harrison, Jo Illiffe, Laurence Keen OBE, the Ven. David Meara, Pauline Sheppard, Tim Tatton Brown, David Thomas, Geoffrey Tyack, and Clive Williams for invaluable advice along the way. Any mistakes are the author's responsibility alone

Illustration & Photo Credits: Bodleian Library, University of Oxford, 1 (225.469), 4, 10, 11 (225.419), 27 (GM1.41va); by permission of the British Library, London, 20 (Harl. 965.f.253), 21(Harl,965 f.254), 22 (Harl, 965.f.256); reproduced by kind permission of Berkshire Record Office, Scale Drawings by Thomas Goodman and 29 (G422); ©National Portrait Gallery, 34 (D5436); Copyright Reading Museum (Reading Borough Council), 5 (REDMG:1970.31.1); by kind permission of Wiltshire and Swindon Archives, iv; Michael Miller, 3, 6, 8, 9, 14, 15, 16, 18, 23, 24, 25, 26, 28, 31, 32, 33, outside front cover, outside back cover, top; David Thomas, 19, Outside Cover Bottom; Author 7, 13, 17. The Millennium Tapestry: Chair of Millennium Group, Heather Macaulay, designed by Tony Driver, sewn by Sarah Thomas, Lily Rennie, Ann Disney, Julie Heel, Mary Illife, Peter Robinson

Bibliography and References: These have been appended to a copy of this publication which has been lodged with the Berkshire Record Office.

ISBN NO 978-0-9933135-0